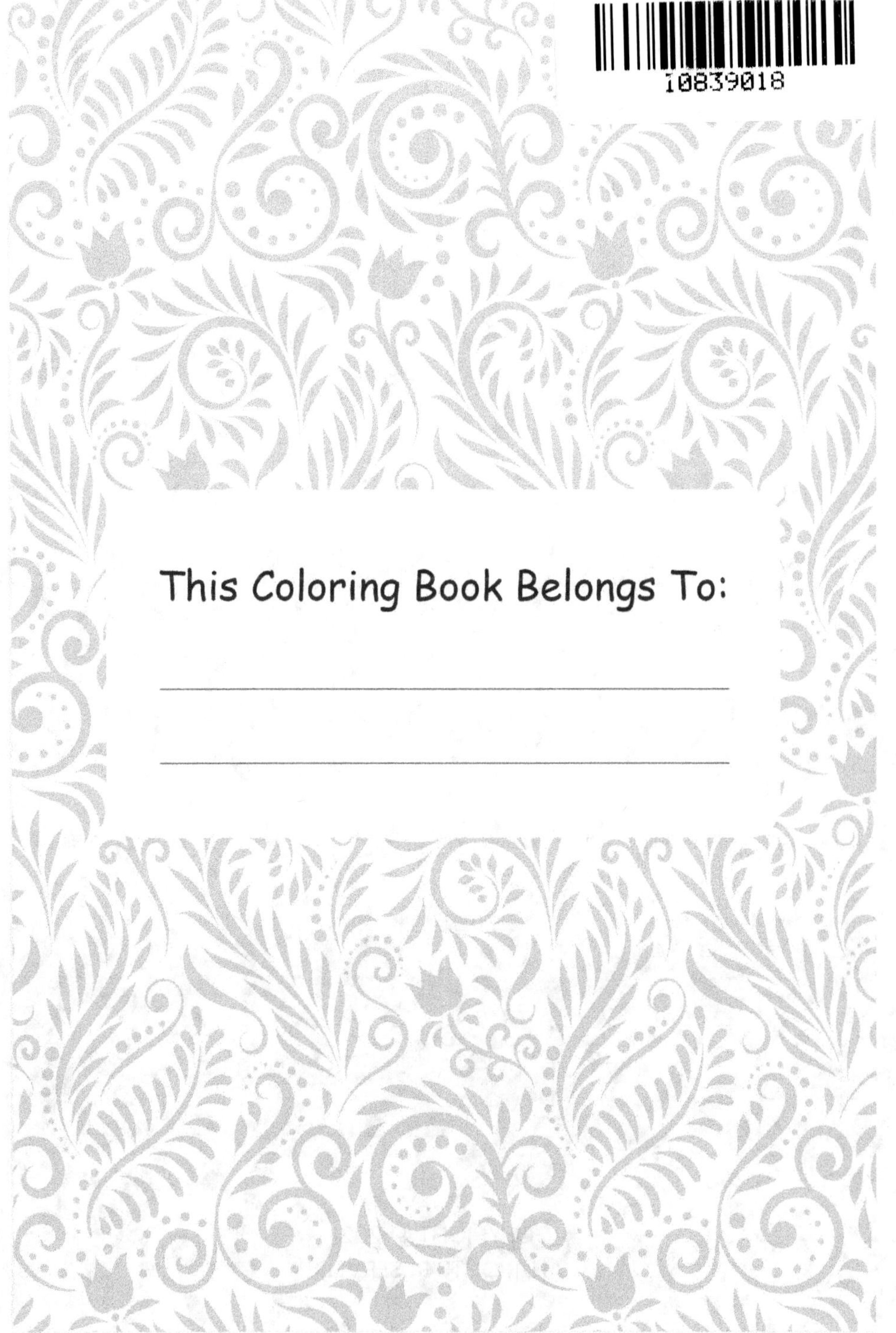

This Coloring Book Belongs To:

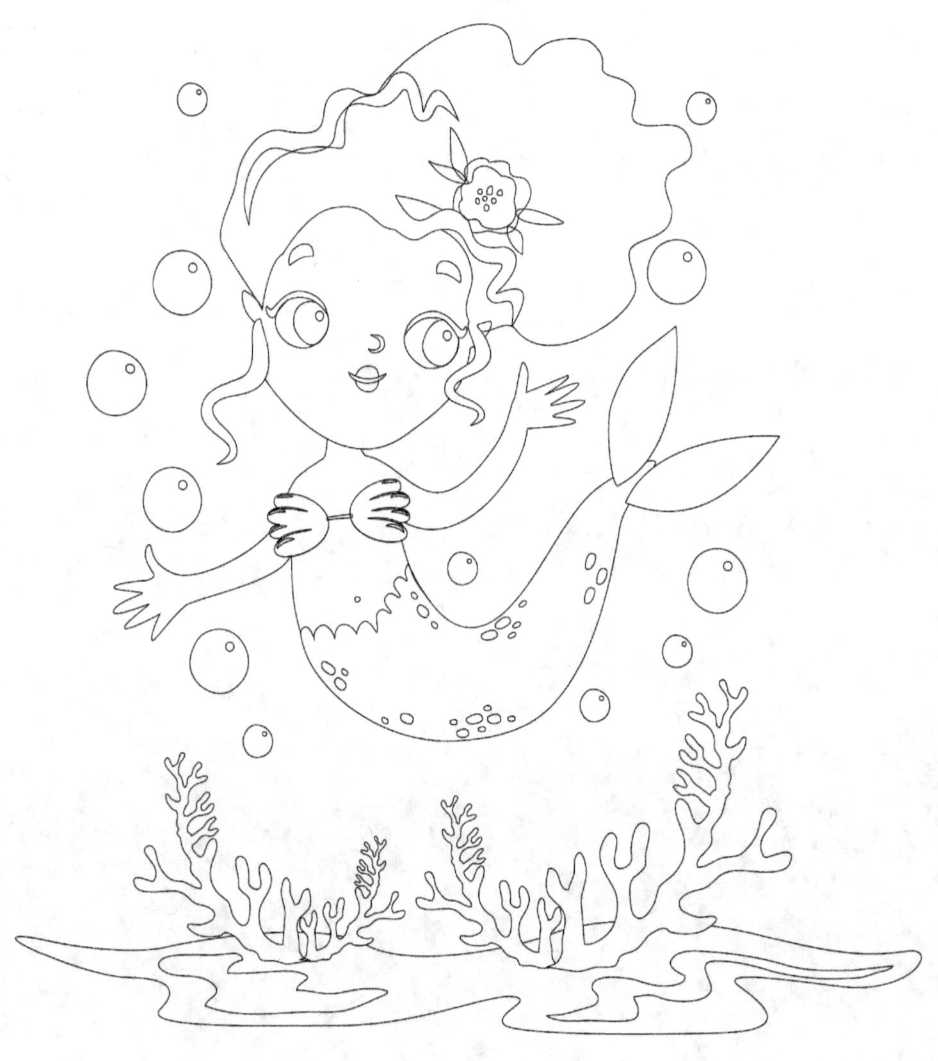

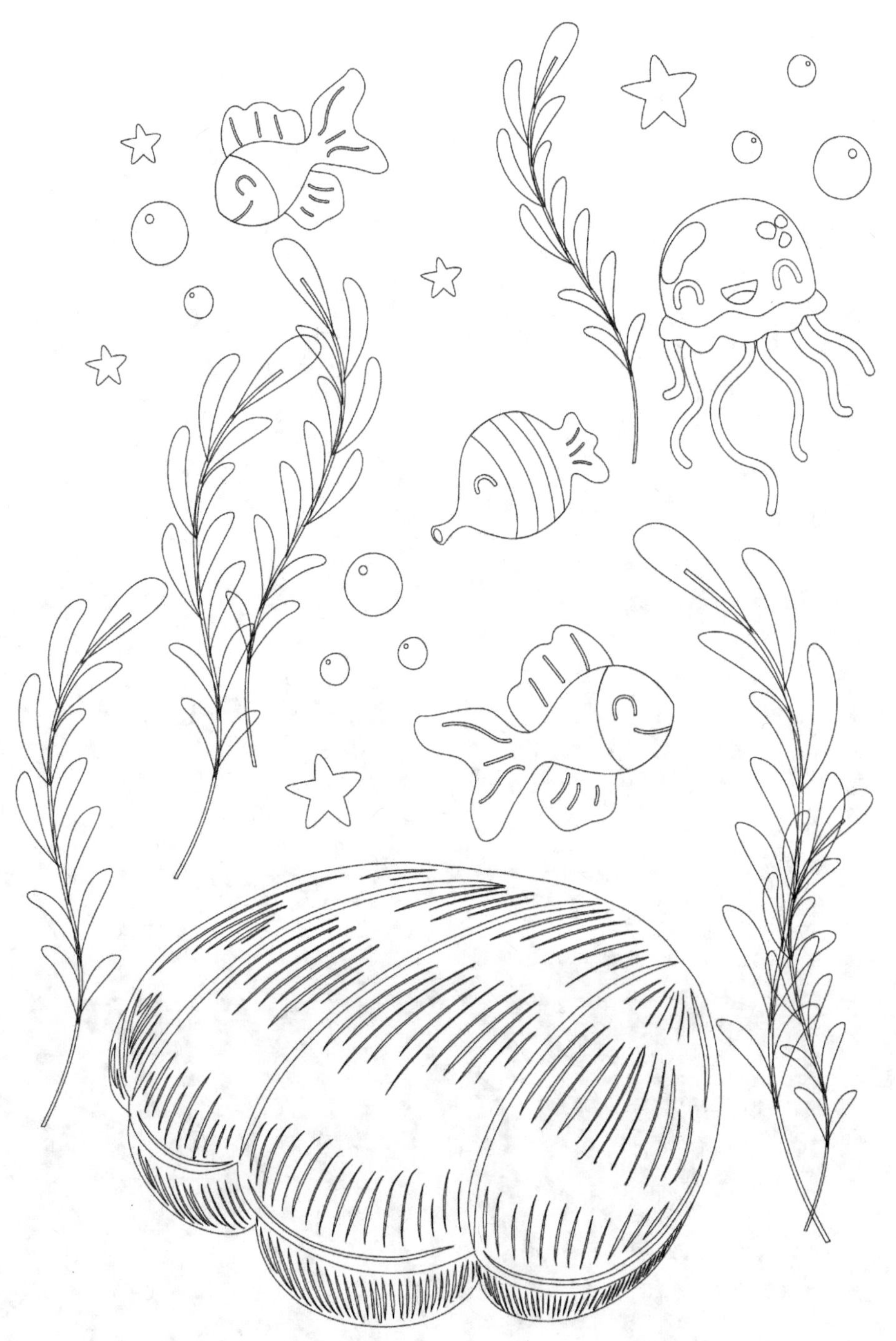

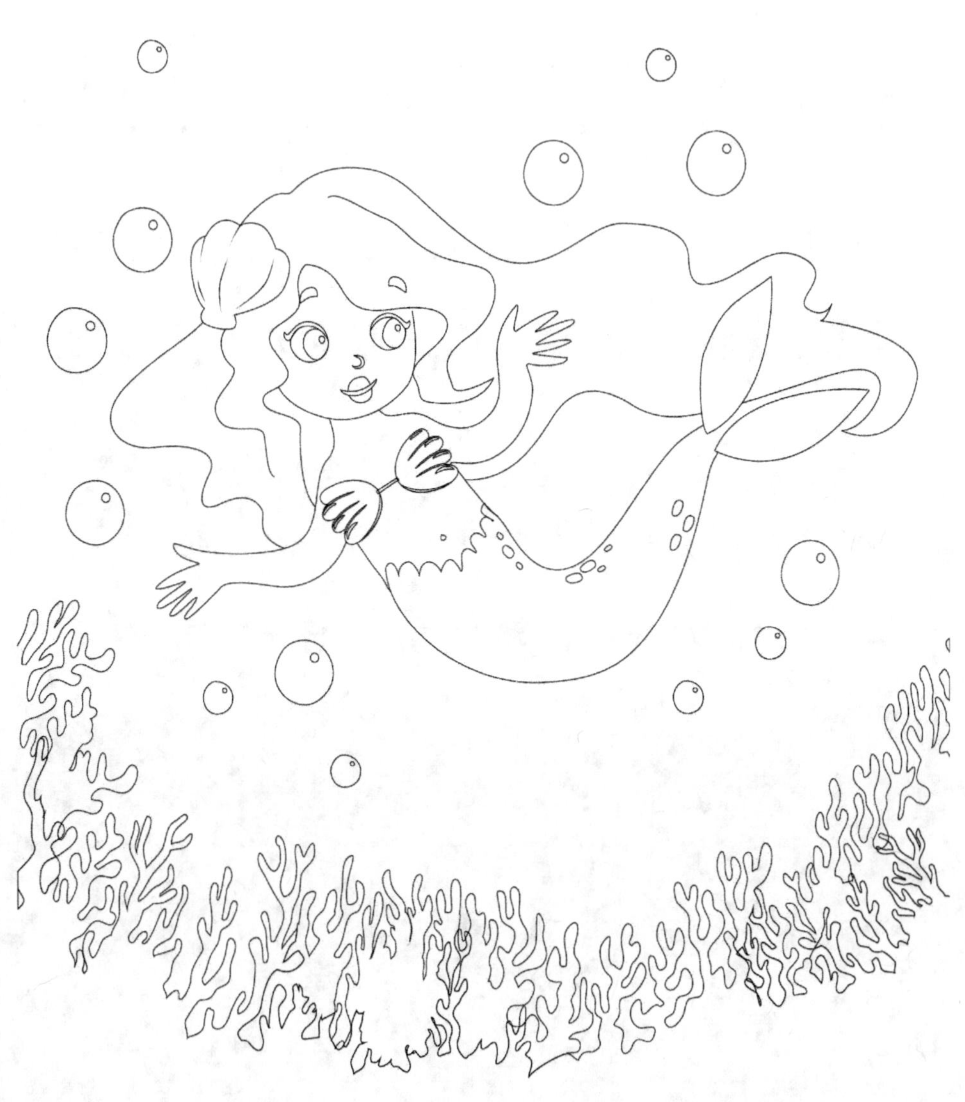

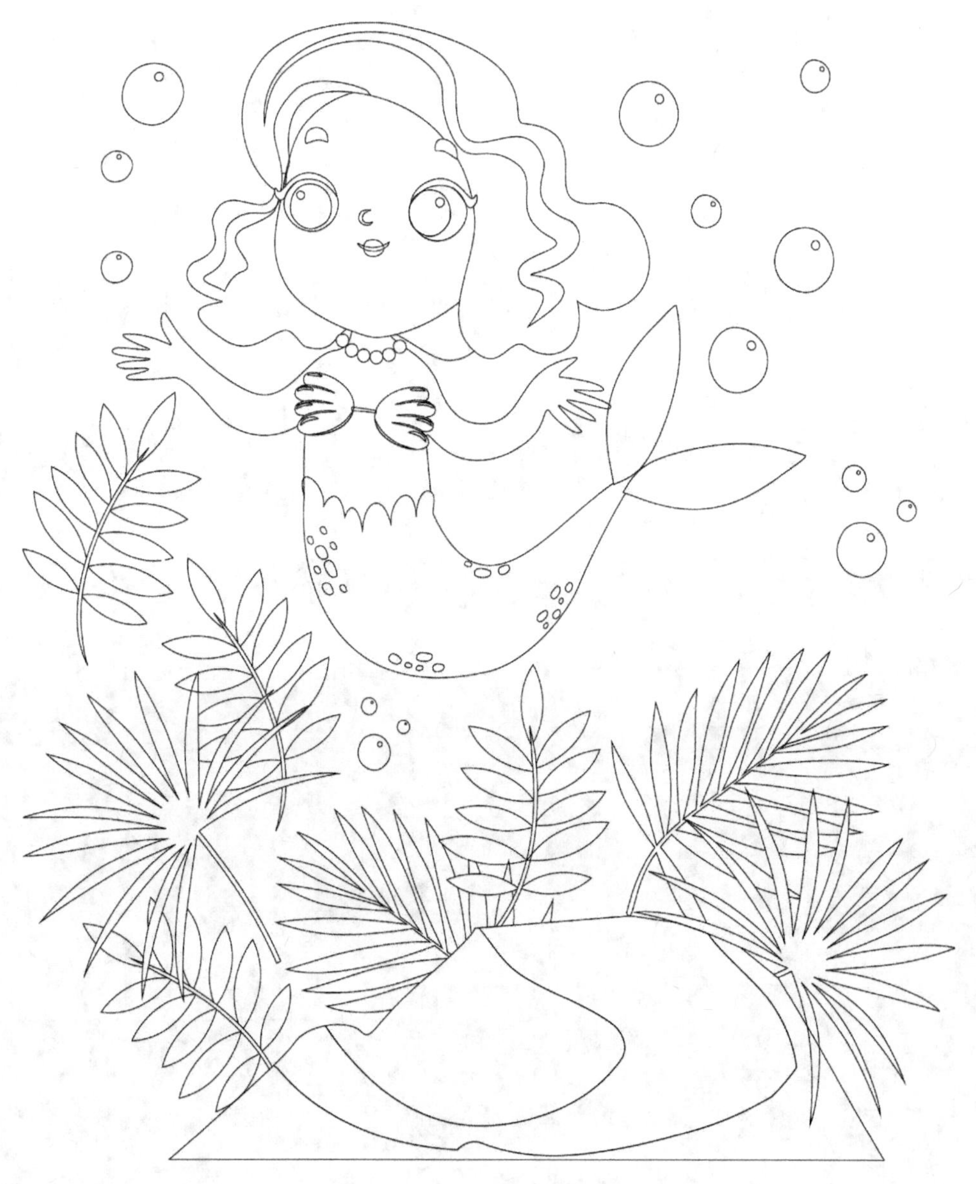

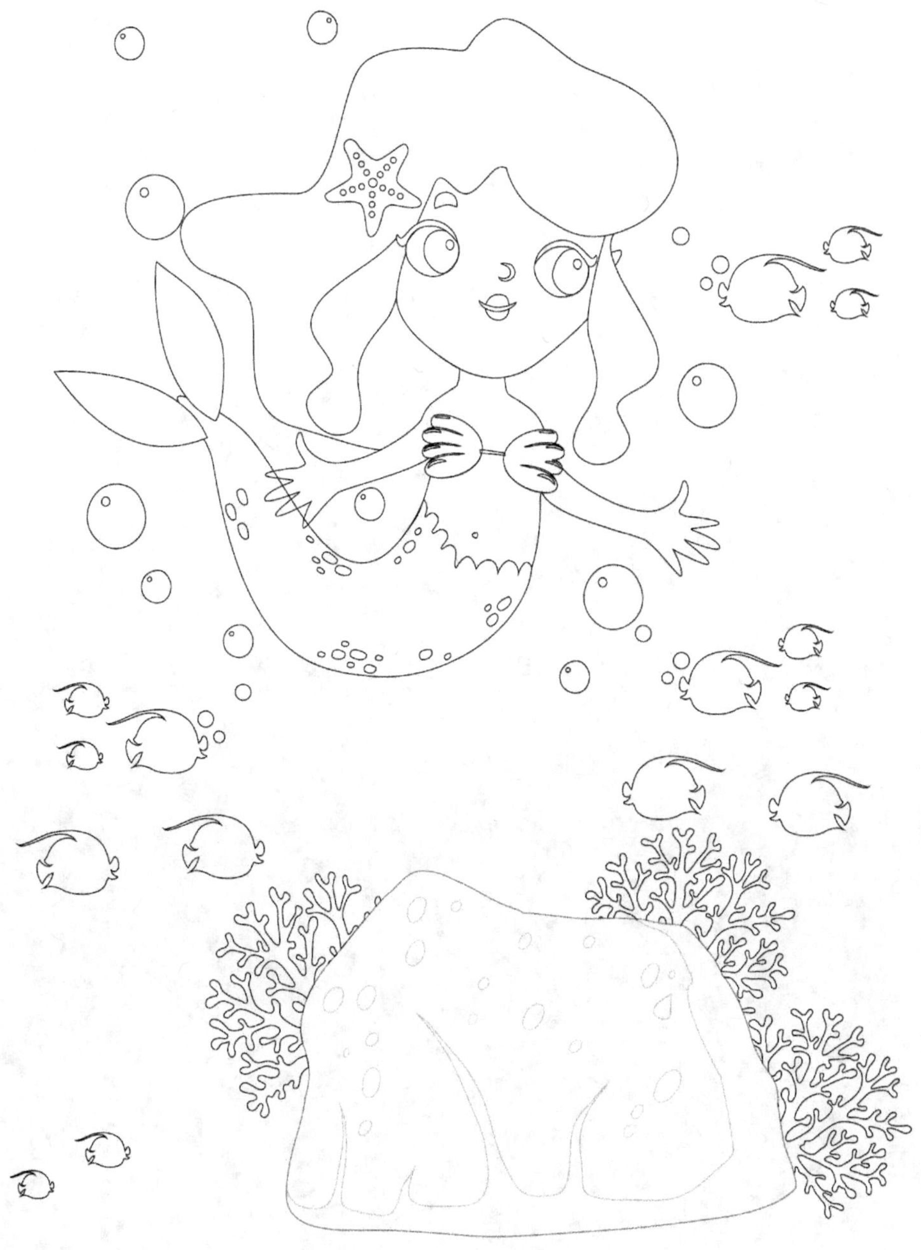

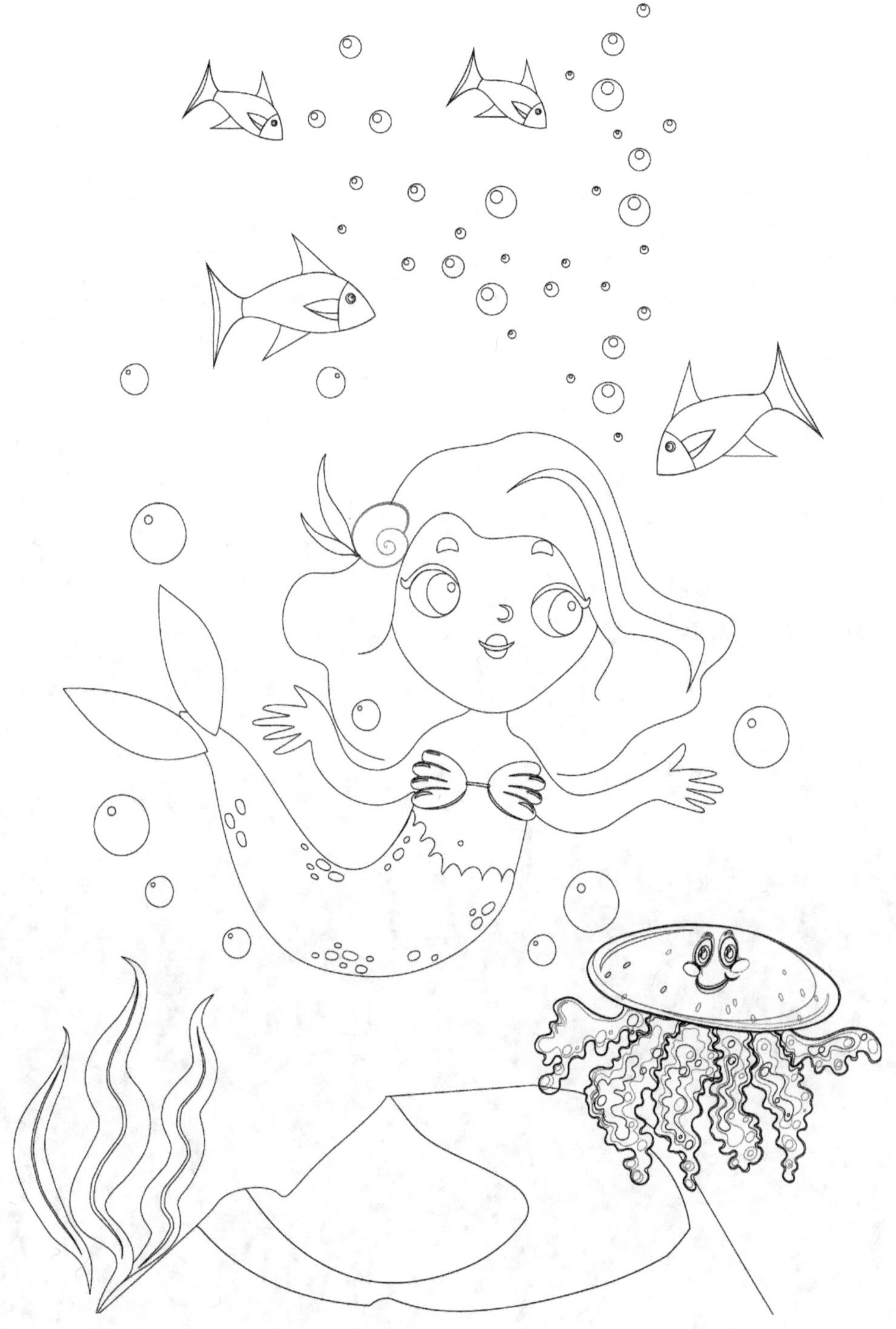

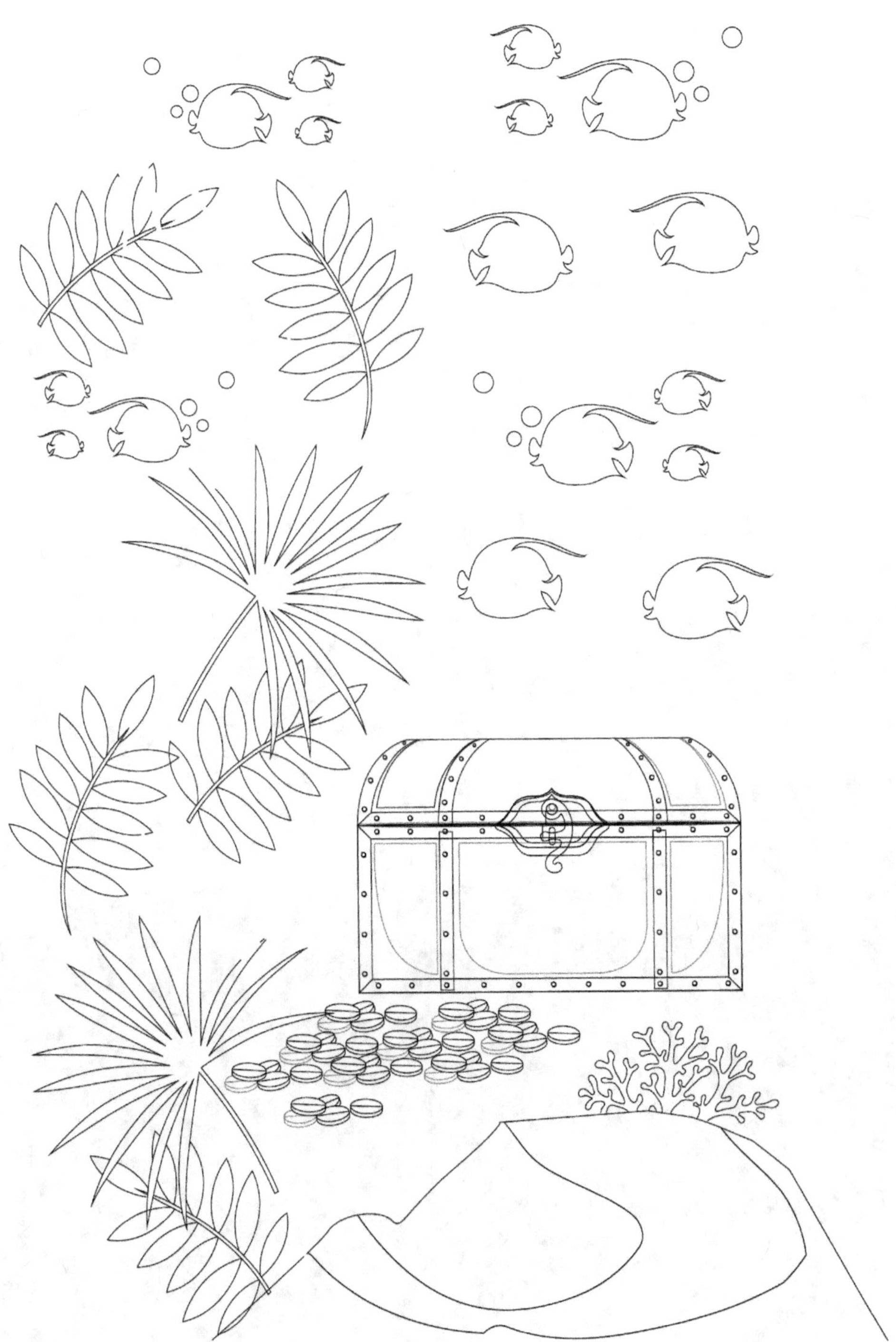

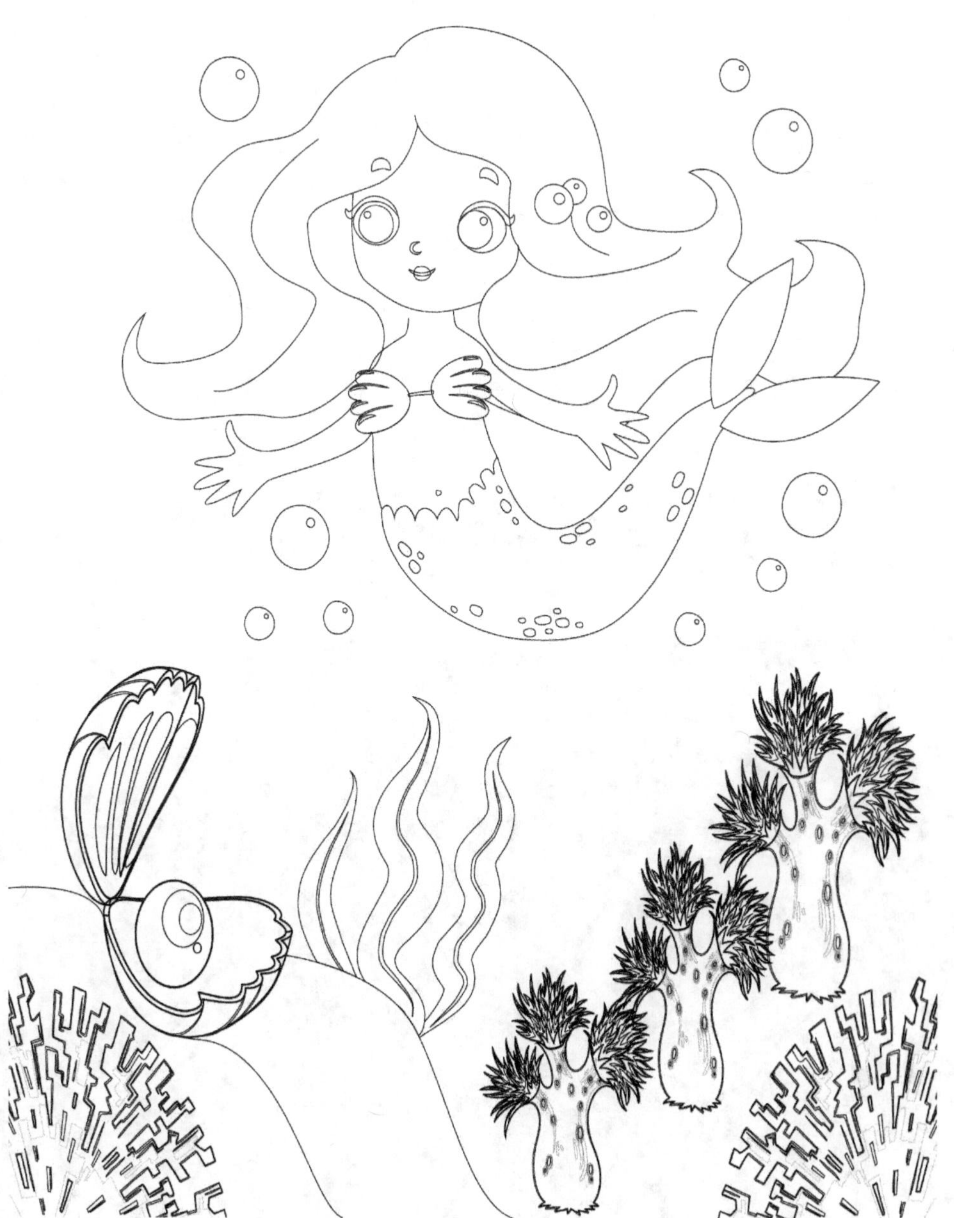

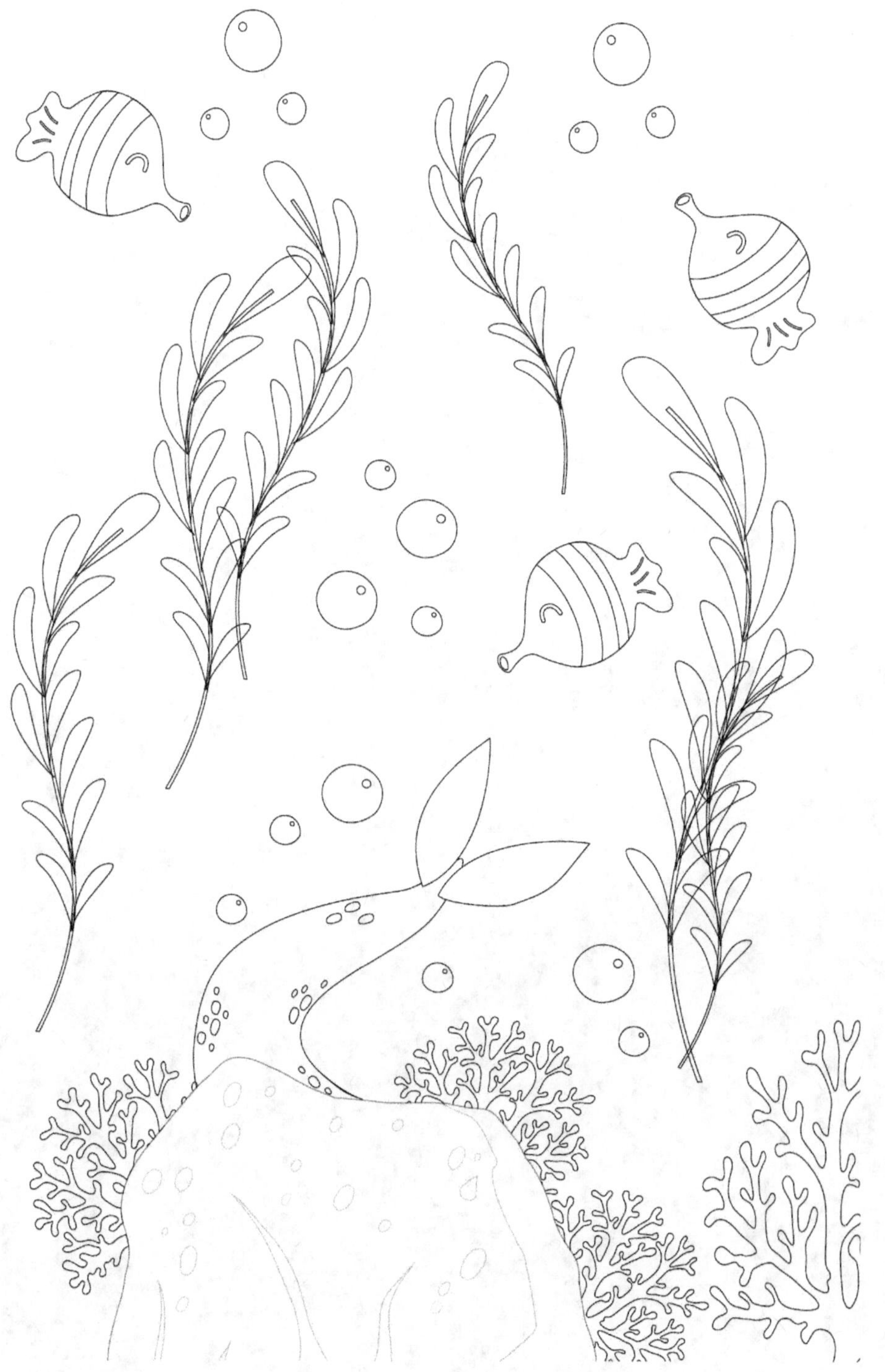

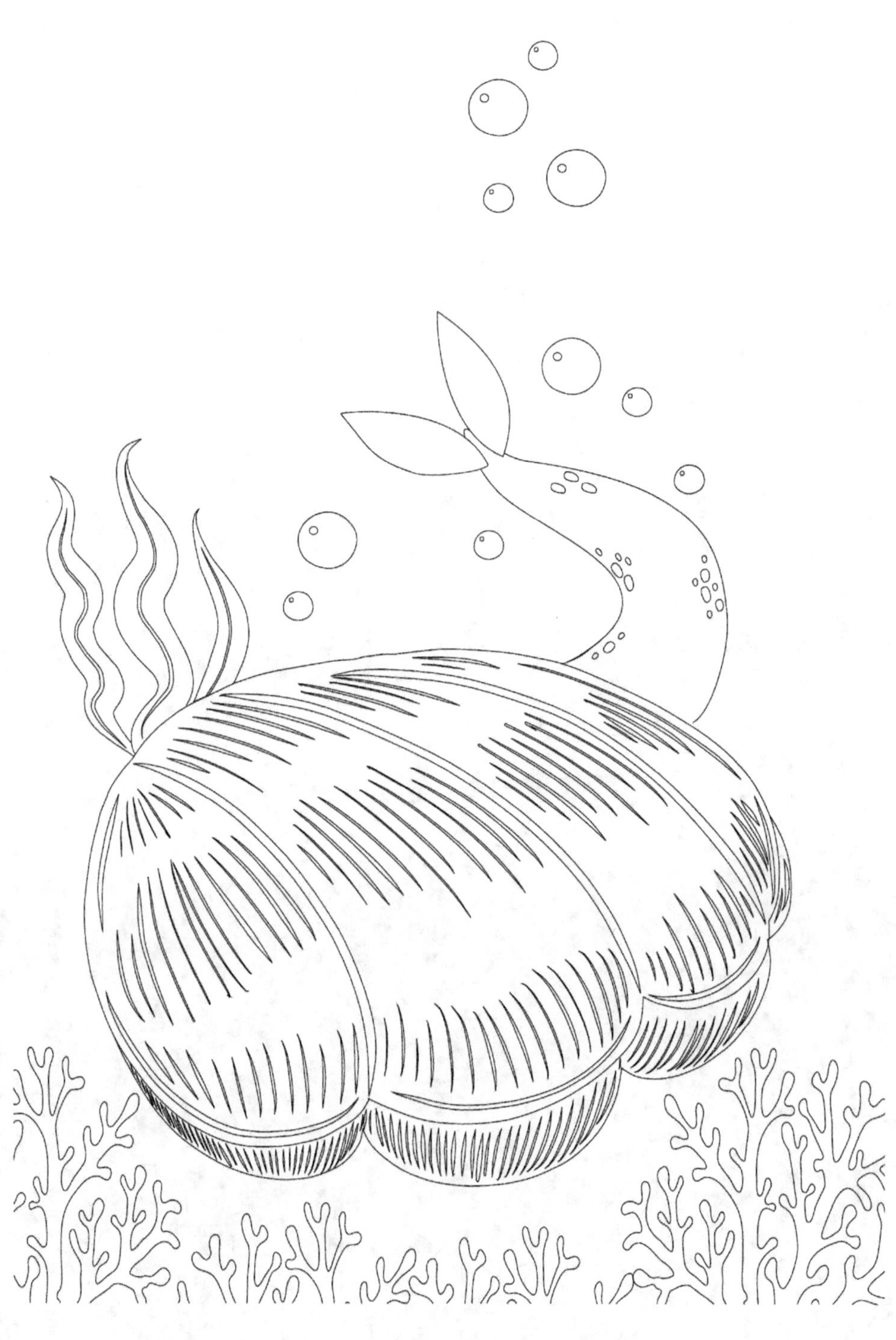

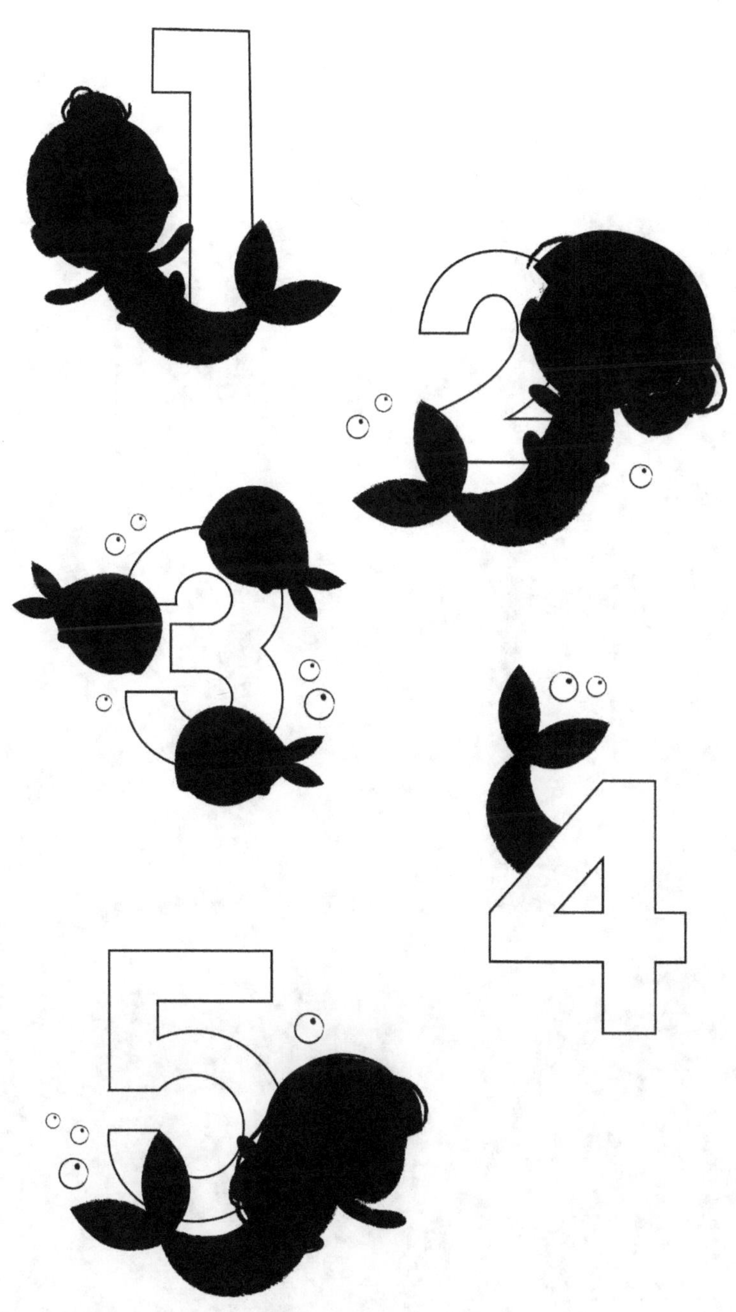

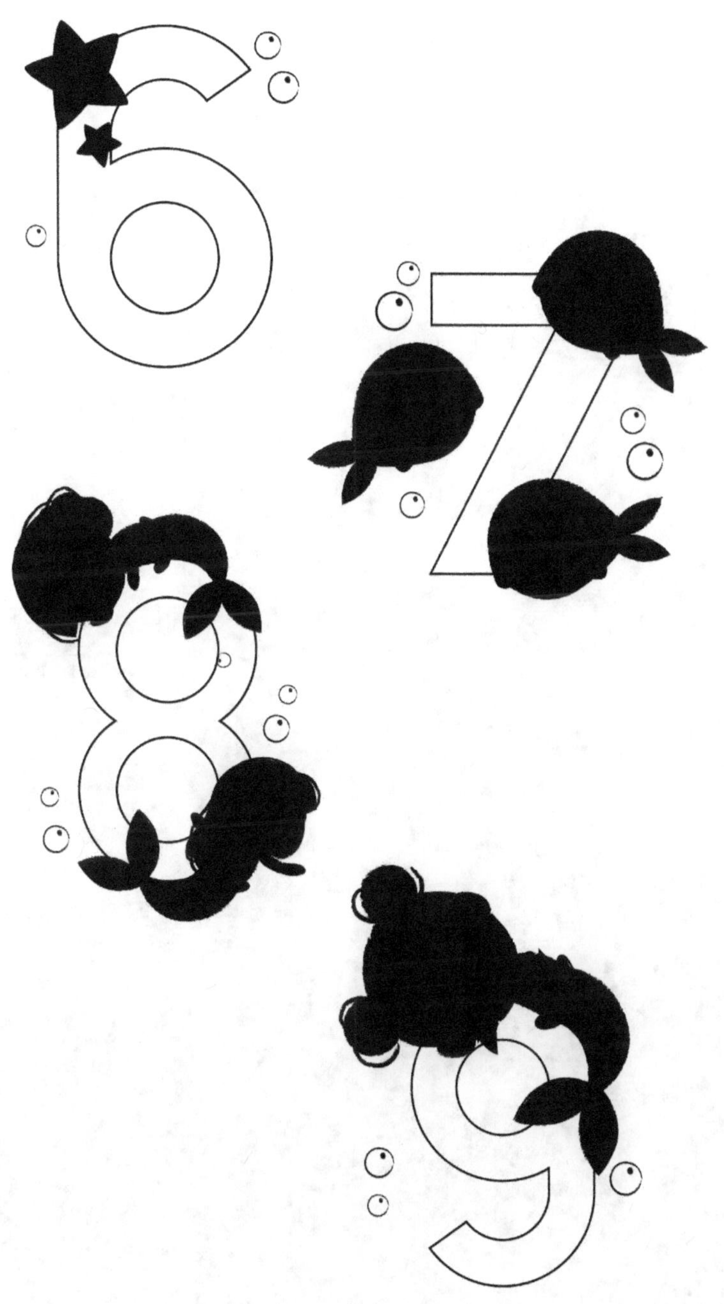

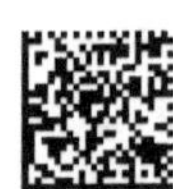

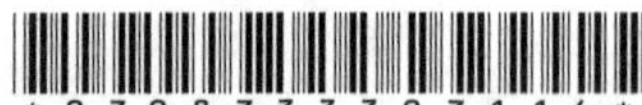